*Author:*

**Ian Graham** earned a diploma in applied physics at City University, London. He then earned a graduate degree in journalism. Since becoming a freelance author and journalist, he has written more than 250 children's nonfiction books.

*Series creator:*

**David Salariya** was born in Dundee, Scotland. He has illustrated a wide range of books and has created and designed many new series for publishers in the UK and overseas. David established The Salariya Book Company in 1989. He lives in Brighton, England, with his wife, illustrator Shirley Willis, and their son, Jonathan.

*Artists:*

**Bryan Beach**
**David Pavon**
**Caroline Romanet**
**Andy Rowland**
**Paco Sordo**
**Diego Vaisberg**

*Editor:*

**Jacqueline Ford**

© The Salariya Book Company Ltd MMXVIII

Published in Great Britain in 2018 by
**The Salariya Book Company Ltd**
25 Marlborough Place, Brighton BN1 1UB

ISBN-13: 978-0-531-23143-2 (lib. bdg.) 978-0-531-23238-5 (pbk.)

All rights reserved.
Published in 2018 in the United States
by Franklin Watts
An imprint of Scholastic Inc.

A CIP catalog record for this book is available
from the Library of Congress.

Printed and bound in China.
Printed on paper from sustainable sources.
1 2 3 4 5 6 7 8 9 10 R 27 26 25 24 23 22 21 20 19 18

SCHOLASTIC, FRANKLIN WATTS, and associated logos are trademarks and/or registered trademarks of Scholastic Inc.

PAPER FROM
SUSTAINABLE
FORESTS

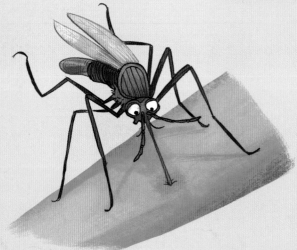

# The Science of Scabs and Pus

# The Sticky Truth About Blood

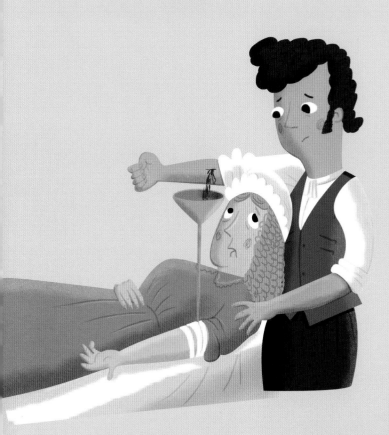

written by
# Ian Graham

Franklin Watts®
An Imprint of Scholastic Inc.

# Contents

# Introduction

We all have blood inside us. It's the red stuff that sometimes drips out of a cut. Blood is constantly on the move, traveling around your body carrying all sorts of useful things the body needs. It also carries heat to keep your fingers and toes warm.

Blood is made mainly of red cells, white cells, and small particles called platelets. Red cells carry oxygen around the body, white cells fight germs, and platelets help to plug leaks in blood vessels. They're carried around the body by a moving stream of watery liquid called plasma. Blood is red because the red cells contain a substance called hemoglobin, and when hemoglobin gets together with oxygen from the lungs, it turns red.

Blood is vital for life. We can't live without it, so the body tries to keep blood safe and clean inside it. You're only likely to see blood if you scrape your knee, cut your finger, or have a nosebleed.

# What Are Blood Groups?

## What IS the Rhesus Factor?

Red blood cells have substances called antigens on their surface. One of these, D antigen, is also called the Rhesus factor because it was discovered in Rhesus monkeys. People who have it are Rhesus positive, or RH positive.

## What Are the Main Blood Groups?

All human blood belongs to one of four groups or types, called A, B, AB, and O. This way of dividing blood into groups is called the ABO system. The most common of these four blood groups is O. About half of all people have group O blood.

All human blood looks the same, but it isn't the same. There are different types of blood, called blood groups. Everyone's blood belongs to one of these groups. Most of the time it doesn't matter which blood group you have. But if you have to be given extra blood in the hospital, it's important that doctors know which group you have so that they can give you the correct blood.

The rarest of the eight main blood groups is AB- (AB Rhesus negative). Fewer than one person in a hundred has AB- blood.

## Do Animals Have Blood Groups?

We are not the only creatures to have blood groups. Animals have blood groups, too. Some have a lot. Cows have more than 800 blood groups. More than 13 have been found in dogs. Horses have 30 main blood groups. Cats have only three.

Blood carries all kinds of useful substances around the body, including vitamins, chemical messengers called hormones, and tiny traces of minerals and elements—including gold!

## Helpful Hint

If you have group O blood, look out for mosquitoes and keep some insect spray handy. Research has shown that bloodsucking mosquitoes bite people with group O blood more often than they bite other people.

# What Does the Heart Do?

The heart's job is to push blood around the body. It's a big squishy living pump made of muscle. You don't have to think about using it, because it keeps on working all the time, day and night. Luckily, it's made of a special type of muscle that doesn't get tired, so it never has to stop for a rest. Your heart normally beats about 70 times a minute. When your muscles have to work harder, they need more oxygen. Your heart beats faster to send more blood around the body and give the muscles the extra oxygen they need.

## Where Is the Heart?

Nearly all people have their heart on the left side of their chest. About one person in 10,000 has the heart on the other side of the chest. This vital organ, about the size of a clenched fist, is protected by a bony cage formed by the ribs.

## How Does the Heart Pump?

Squeezing a plastic water bottle squirts water out. The heart pumps blood in the same way. It takes in blood from the lungs and squeezes to pump it around the body. When the blood returns to the heart, it's sent to the lungs to collect the oxygen you breathe in and then it's pumped around the body again.

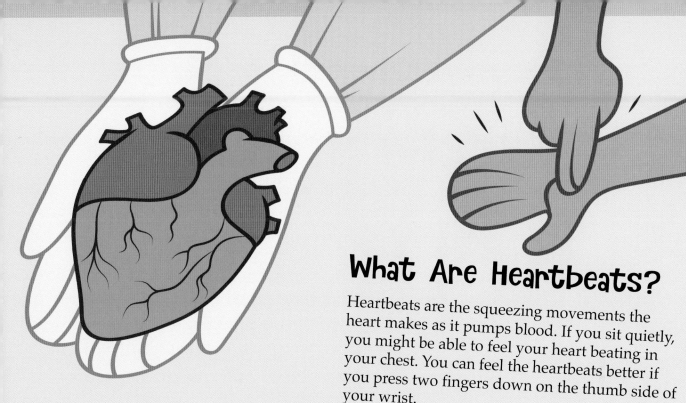

## What Are Heartbeats?

Heartbeats are the squeezing movements the heart makes as it pumps blood. If you sit quietly, you might be able to feel your heart beating in your chest. You can feel the heartbeats better if you press two fingers down on the thumb side of your wrist.

The heart is a remarkable organ. It beats about 100,000 times every day. In an average lifetime, the heart will beat an amazing 2.5 billion times.

## Can You Believe It?

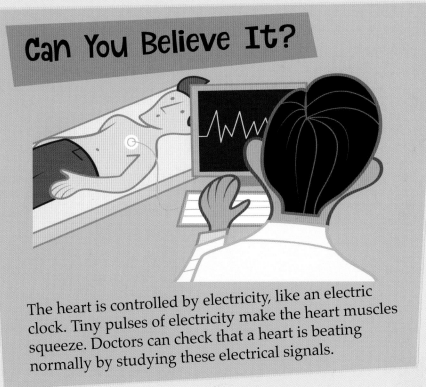

The heart is controlled by electricity, like an electric clock. Tiny pulses of electricity make the heart muscles squeeze. Doctors can check that a heart is beating normally by studying these electrical signals.

# How Does Blood Move Around the Body?

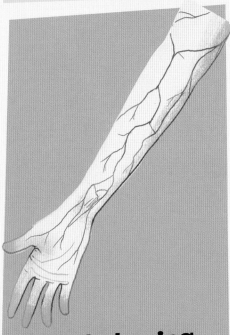

Blood doesn't slosh around inside your body. It moves, or circulates, through tubes called blood vessels. They connect the heart to nearly every part of the body. There are big blood vessels thicker than your thumb, and tiny blood vessels so small that you'd need a microscope to see them. The vessels that carry blood away from the heart to the rest of the body are called arteries. Another set of vessels called veins collects blood from the body and carries it back to the heart.

## Are Arteries and Veins Different?

Arteries have strong, thick walls to withstand the force of blood being forced through them by the heart. Veins feel less of the heart's pushing force, so their walls are thinner. Veins are often closer to the skin's surface, so you might be able to see them. They look like blue lines.

## What Are Capillaries?

Capillaries are tiny blood vessels that connect arteries to veins. Their walls are so thin that oxygen can pass through them into the body's cells. Capillaries are usually too small to see, but if they swell up, leak, or break they can sometimes make spidery streaks in the skin. Broken capillaries can be caused by extreme temperature changes.

10

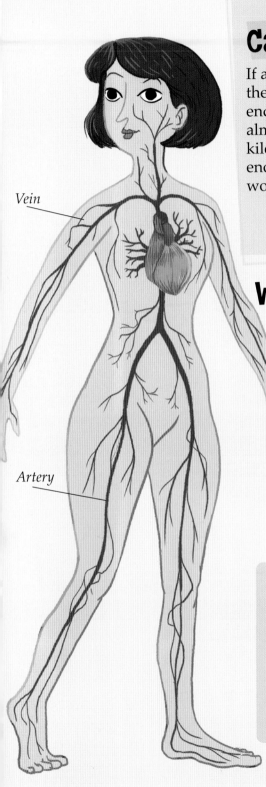

*Vein*

*Artery*

## Can You Believe It?

If all the blood vessels in the human body were laid end to end, they would be almost 60,000 miles (100,000 kilometers) long. That's enough to go around the world two and a half times!

## Why Do You Blush?

Blushing, or getting red in the face, happens when your brain sends out a message that makes capillaries in the skin open wider. Extra blood flowing through them turns the skin red. Blushing affects the face because the skin there has lots of capillaries close to the surface.

Blood takes less than a minute to travel from the heart, all the way around the body, and back to the heart again.

## Where Does Pus Come From?

If your body finds an infection, it sends an army of white blood cells to fight the germs. The white cells engulf the germs and then die. Each white cell is too small to see, but when millions of them gather together they form creamy white pus.

OK, I'm sending in the army!

# What Is Pus?

If you have a cut and you don't keep it clean, it might become infected. You'll know it's infected if you see thick, sticky, white or yellow goo oozing out of it. This yucky stuff is called pus, and it comes from blood. Pus is good and bad. It's good because it shows that your body is fighting an infection, but it's bad because it shows that you didn't keep a cut clean, you have an infection, and pus is pretty disgusting stuff.

There are several different types of white blood cells. The most common are called neutrophils, the white blood cells that form pus.

## What Is an Abscess?

If pus gets trapped inside the body, it makes a swollen lump called an abscess. Most abscesses are caused when germs infect part of the body and then the body fights back. If an abscess forms just under the skin, it might make a lump big enough to see.

Always wash your hands before and after touching an abscess to prevent the spread of infection, and never try to pop or squeeze it.

## What Is a Zit?

Pus may have no smell at all, or it may be very stinky indeed. The smell depends on the type of bacteria that caused the infection.

The skin is covered with small holes called pores. If dead skin cells block a pore, an oily substance called sebum is trapped inside. Bacteria multiply in the sebum. When the blood sends white cells to fight the bacteria, they form the pus that makes a pustule, also called a pimple or zit.

## Disgusting Data

Before doctors found out what caused infections, they thought pus was part of the normal healing process. They thought creamy pus was good, but bad-smelling pus was a sign that something had gone wrong.

13

# What Is a Scab?

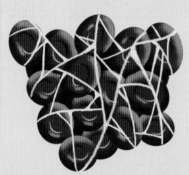

## What Is a Clot?

The first step in healing damaged skin is to stop blood from leaking out. Platelets and red blood cells stick together in the cut. The blood also forms hairlike strands of a substance called fibrin. They clump together to make a gooey blob called a clot, which plugs the cut.

Your skin is amazing stuff. It's very good at healing itself. As soon as skin is scraped or cut, your body gets to work repairing the damage. You don't have to give it a moment's thought, because your body does it all by itself. Blood is the body's secret weapon when it comes to fixing this damage. When it gets to work on broken skin, the repair job it does produces a crusty patch on top of the skin. That's called a scab.

The strands of fibrin that help to form a scab are made from a substance called fibrinogen that is made by the liver and carried around the body by the blood.

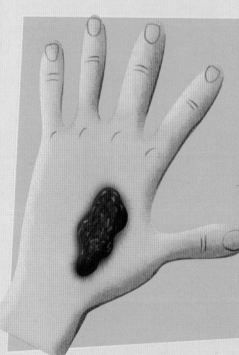

## Why Are Scabs Crusty?

The blood clot that plugs a cut soon dries up and hardens. It forms a crusty scab over the cut. It looks gross, but underneath it, out of sight, new skin is growing across the cut. The scab protects the new skin. When the scab's job is done, it falls off.

Cool knee patches!

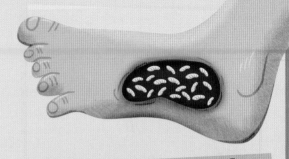

## Disgusting Data

When a wound will not heal, doctors sometimes treat it by putting wriggling, wormlike maggots on it! Maggots are baby flies. The maggots eat dead flesh, leaving clean, healthy flesh that heals better.

Maggots have been used to clean out wounds and help them to heal for at least a thousand years, and probably a lot longer than that.

## Is It OK to Pick Scabs?

It's very tempting to pick at a scab, especially if it's itchy, but try not to pick it. If you pull a scab off before the skin has healed, the cut will start bleeding again and you'll have to wait for a new scab to form all over again.

15

# What Is a Bruise?

It takes about two weeks for the blood that forms a bruise to break down and for the bruise to fade away and finally disappear.

## What Is a Black Eye?

Your eyes sit inside sockets made of bone. If something hits an eye socket hard, some of the blood vessels there may be crushed against the bone and break. Blood leaks out and makes a bruise around the eye. The dark bruise is called a black eye.

When blood leaks out of blood vessels and gets trapped under the skin, it makes a colorful mark called a bruise. A bruise might be caused by a fall or bump that breaks small blood vessels and lets blood leak out. Bruises can be painful, because the leaking blood causes a swelling that presses on nerve cells in the skin. When a bruise heals and the swelling goes down, the pain goes away, too. Blood vessels break and burst more easily as you get older, so older people bruise more easily than children.

Ouch!

It's nearly gone!

# Why Do Bruises Change Color?

You can guess the age of a bruise by its color. A new bruise looks black or blue, but it doesn't stay like that for long. The blood cells trapped under the skin quickly start breaking down, and as they break down they change color. The dark colors soon fade to yellow and brown, and then disappear.

# Can You Always See a Bruise?

Some bruises are invisible, because they are deep inside the body where you can't see them. Internal organs like the heart, liver, and kidneys can be bruised. In fact, any part of the body with a blood supply can be bruised. It's even possible to bruise your brain.

To help reduce swelling or the amount of bruising after an injury, apply a cold compress to the bruise for at least 10 minutes.

# Fascinating Fact

Some marks on the skin look like bruises, but they are actually a type of birthmark. They happen where a patch of skin has lots of extra blood vessels, or vessels that are bigger than normal.

17

# How Does the Body Keep Blood Clean?

## How Does the Liver Clean Blood?

The liver is an amazing living chemical laboratory. As blood flows through it, the liver traps old blood cells and chemicals dissolved in the blood. Then it breaks them down into simpler chemicals that the body can either use or get rid of when you go to the bathroom.

Blood collects waste materials from the body, and this waste has to be removed somehow. If your body wasn't able to do it, the waste would build up and make you sick. This cleaning work is done by the liver and kidneys. When blood flows through them, they filter out all the bad stuff, leaving clean blood to go around the body again. If you place your hand on your belly, on the right side of your body below your ribs, that's where most of your liver is. Your kidneys are on either side of your back, below your ribs.

## What Do the Kidneys Do?

A human body has two kidneys. Each kidney contains a million tiny filters called nephrons. As blood passes through them, they filter water out of it, remove waste materials dissolved in it, and return some of the water to the blood. The watery waste forms urine, which you pee out.

The liver is a very important organ, because it does hundreds of different jobs. These include the removal of all sorts of particles, waste materials, and chemicals from the blood.

## What Is Dialysis?

If the kidneys stop working, a machine can do their job instead. In a hospital or clinic, the machine takes in blood from a patient, filters it, and then sends the clean blood back into the patient's body. Using a kidney machine to clean blood like this is called dialysis.

The liver is the only organ in the body that can grow back if part of it has to be removed by doctors because of damage or disease.

## Can You Believe It?

If your liver isn't working well, you might turn yellow. It happens because a substance called bilirubin, made by old blood cells breaking down in the liver, leaks into the blood and turns the skin yellow.

# What Is Anemia?

Red blood cell

Oxygen molecule

## Why Is Hemoglobin Important?

Hemoglobin is the substance that enables blood to carry oxygen. It's a big molecule called a protein. Hemoglobin contains iron, and it's the iron that grabs oxygen as the blood flows through the lungs. When the normally dark red hemoglobin picks up oxygen, it changes to bright red.

Blood can have problems, or disorders, that stop it from working at its best. The most common blood disorder is anemia. Someone with anemia has blood that doesn't carry enough oxygen around the body. There can be several reasons for this. It might be because there aren't enough red cells in the blood, or it might be because the red cells don't contain enough hemoglobin. Whatever the cause, anemia starves the body's cells of the oxygen they need, which means they aren't able to work properly.

# How Does Anemia Make You Feel?

Anemia can make you feel tired and weak, and you might look pale. You might be short of breath or feel dizzy. Other illnesses can cause these problems, too, so the only way to make sure that anemia is the cause is to have a blood test.

Anemia is one of the most widespread health problems today. About 1.6 billion people, or a quarter of the world's population, have it.

# What Is Sickle Cell Anemia?

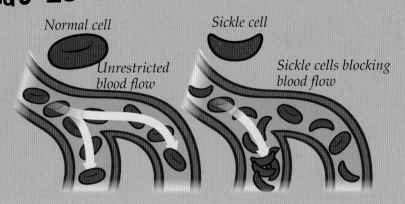

Normal cell

Unrestricted blood flow

Sickle cell

Sickle cells blocking blood flow

Healthy red blood cells are disc-shaped, thin in the middle, and thick around the edge. They slip through blood vessels easily. People who have sickle cell anemia have red blood cells that are banana-shaped. These abnormal cells don't live long and they get stuck in blood vessels, blocking blood flow.

A single tiny droplet of blood just one twenty-fifth of an inch (1 millimeter) across contains up to 5 million red cells, 10,000 white cells, and 400,000 platelets.

# Fascinating Fact

Anemia may leave telltale signs in the patient's bones. Scientists have found these signs in ancient skeletons. The oldest known case of anemia was found in skeletons of people who died 4,000 years ago.

# What Is Hemophilia?

The most common type of hemophilia is called hemophilia A. People with hemophilia A have too little clotting factor 8 in their blood.

The blood's ability to make clots that stop bleeding can sometimes go wrong. Your blood contains substances called clotting factors that help to make clots when they're needed. People with a rare condition called hemophilia don't have enough of these clotting factors. Their blood takes a long time to clot, so they bleed more than normal. They don't just bleed from cuts. They can also bleed inside their body. Hemophilia is passed on from parents to their children. Because of the way it's passed on, boys are much more likely than girls to get it.

# How Is Hemophilia Treated?

Healthy blood contains 13 clotting factors. All of them are needed for blood to clot as it should. Having too little of just one of them can stop blood from clotting normally. People with hemophilia are treated with injections of the clotting factor they lack.

# How Do Mosquitoes Stop Blood From Clotting?

Bloodsucking mosquitoes have to stop their victims' blood from clotting so they can suck it up. When a mosquito lands on you, it pushes a needle-shaped mouthpart called a proboscis through your skin and injects some spit. The spit contains a substance called an anticoagulant that keeps the blood runny.

# What Is a Carrier?

Girls rarely have hemophilia, but cells in their body can contain the faulty instructions that cause the illness. Even though they seem perfectly healthy, they can still pass on hemophilia to their children. People who pass on an illness without having it themselves are called carriers.

## Fascinating Fact

Britain's Queen Victoria (1819–1901) was a hemophilia carrier. She passed hemophilia on to some of her children. They married into the royal families of Europe and passed hemophilia on to their own children and grandchildren.

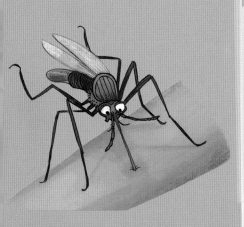

# What Is Leukemia?

The word leukemia comes from Greek words that mean "white" and "blood." People with leukemia have an excess of white blood cells that cause them to become sick.

Your body is busy making billions of new blood cells every day. The instructions for making them are stored in a substance called DNA found inside cells. Sometimes, in rare cases, a mistake in the instructions leads to the body making too many white cells. The extra cells do not grow properly, so they can't fight infections. There are so many faulty white cells that they stop the healthy blood cells from working well, too. The result is a disease called leukemia.

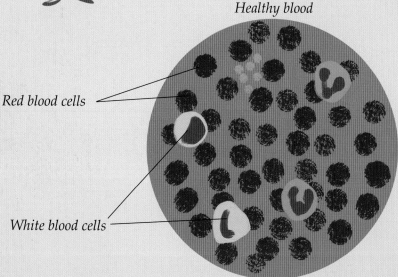

*Healthy blood*

Red blood cells

White blood cells

*Blood of leukemia patient*

*Increased number of white blood cells*

# How Is Leukemia Treated?

One way to treat leukemia is to use medicine to kill the white blood cells that aren't working properly. The medicine could be given as pills to swallow or as a liquid injected into a vein. The liquid treatment is called chemotherapy.

# What Is Radiotherapy?

Radiation is sometimes used to treat leukemia by killing all the blood-making cells deep in the bone marrow. The patient lies on a bed while a machine moves around firing a beam of radiation at precise places on the body. Using radiation to treat people like this is called radiotherapy.

# What Is a Stem Cell Transplant?

When a leukemia patient's bone marrow cells have been killed by radiation, they have to be replaced by new blood-making cells. These are collected from a healthy person and given to the patient through a drip. The bag of stem cells looks just like a bag of blood.

# Fascinating Fact

Polish scientist Marie Curie (1867–1934) died of leukemia caused by her work. She was one of the first people to study radioactivity, but she didn't know about its dangers. Radiation damaged her bone marrow, causing leukemia.

# What Is a Blood Transfusion?

## What Is Crossmatching?

Hospitals check that blood is safe to give to a patient by crossmatching. Some of the replacement blood is mixed with the watery part of the patient's blood. If lumps form, the two bloods do not match. If there are no lumps, the bloods match and it's safe to do the transfusion.

The human body is very good at making new blood to replace small blood losses. Sometimes, though, someone loses so much blood so quickly that the body can't replace it fast enough. Then the person needs to receive extra blood. This is called a blood transfusion. It's vital that the patient is given the correct type of blood. If the wrong blood group is given, the body may treat the new blood like an invading infection and fight it. The result may be that blood clots form inside blood vessels and block them, causing serious damage or even death.

## How Is a Blood Transfusion Given?

Most blood transfusions are given in the hospital. A bag of blood is hung upside down above the patient. The blood flows from the bag along a tube to a hollow needle in the patient's arm. The blood slowly drips straight into a vein and mixes with the patient's own blood.

# Can People Be Given an Animal's Blood?

Hundreds of years ago, doctors tried to take blood from animals and give it to people. They didn't understand that there are different types, or groups, of blood and that they must not be mixed. People who were given transfusions of animal blood sometimes died as a result.

Some doctors specialize in studying blood and treating disorders of the blood. The study of blood is called hematology and blood specialists are called hematologists.

## Fascinating Fact

James Blundell (1790–1878) carried out the first successful blood transfusion in 1818. He had seen women bleed to death in childbirth and wanted to help them. He gave a woman blood from her husband. It worked.

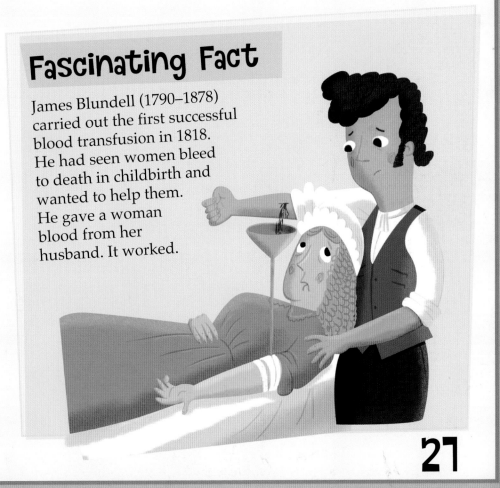

# Why Do People Give Blood?

## How Do You Give Blood?

A nurse pushes a hollow needle into a vein in a donor's arm. Blood flows out of the vein and through a tube to a plastic bag. After a few minutes the bag is full and the needle is pulled out. The tiny needle hole heals very quickly.

The blood used for transfusions comes from blood donors. They are ordinary people who offer to give away some of their blood to help other people. Most adults who are fit and healthy can become blood donors. Every few months they can go to a site near their home. Medical staff check that they are healthy and feeling well, and then they donate some of their blood. One pint of blood is taken from each donor. It's called a unit of blood. After donating, a donor's body quickly makes up more blood until their blood level is back to normal again.

Thousands of units of blood are used every day, and blood cannot be stored for very long, so there is a constant need for blood donations.

# What Happens to Donated Blood?

Blood from a donor is called whole blood, because it contains all its parts. But patients often need only one of the useful things in blood and not the rest. Donated blood can be divided into red cells, white cells, platelets, and plasma. In this way, one unit of blood can help a number of patients.

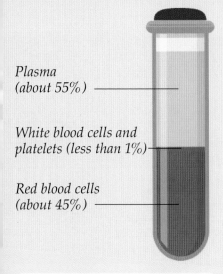

Plasma
(about 55%)

White blood cells and
platelets (less than 1%)

Red blood cells
(about 45%)

Animals can be blood donors, too. With an owner's permission, veterinary surgeons can take some of an animal's blood so that it can be used to help other animals.

# Where Is Donated Blood Kept?

Blood collected from donors is kept in cold stores called blood banks. A blood bank is a giant refrigerator, usually in a hospital. Each bag of blood is labeled with its blood group to make sure that patients who need transfusions are given the correct blood.

## Fascinating Fact

Australian James Harrison has special blood. It contains rare antibodies that can treat an illness called Rhesus disease. If a woman with Rhesus-negative blood is having a baby with Rhesus-positive blood, the mother's body may attack the baby's blood. Injecting the mother with medicine made from Harrison's blood stops this.

# Glossary

**Abscess**  Part of the body that is swollen by a buildup of pus.

**Anemia**  A blood disorder caused by a shortage of red cells or hemoglobin.

**Antigen**  A molecule or substance treated as unwanted or toxic by the body, causing an immune system response.

**Artery**  A blood vessel that carries blood flowing away from the heart.

**Bacteria**  Microscopic single-celled organisms, some of which cause infections and diseases.

**Bilirubin**  An orange-yellow chemical compound found in the liver, produced by the breakdown of old red blood cells.

**Blood clot**  A jellylike blob of blood cells, platelets, and strands of fibrin.

**Blood donor**  Someone who volunteers to give blood to help other people.

**Blood group**  One of the different types of blood, such as those of the ABO system.

**Blood transfusion**  An injection of blood from a healthy person to a patient.

**Bone marrow**  A soft, fatty substance found inside bones that produces blood cells.

**Capillary**  One of the very thin blood vessels that link arteries to veins.

**Clotting factor**  One of the substances in blood that are essential to make the blood clot when necessary.

**Contusion**  Another name for a bruise; skin or another part of the body discolored and swollen by blood leaking from broken blood vessels.

**DNA**  Deoxyribonucleic acid, the molecule that carries the instructions for the growth, development, and functioning of the body's cells.

**Hemophilia**  An inherited blood disorder involving a shortage of one of the clotting factors that makes blood clot, causing excessive bleeding.

**Hormone**  A chemical messenger that circulates in the blood and controls the activity of certain cells or organs.

**Kidney**  One of the two organs that filter waste chemicals out of blood and produce urine.

**Leukemia**  Cancer of the blood, a condition in which the body produces too many white blood cells.

**Liver**  A large organ with hundreds of functions including many concerned with removing waste from the blood, breaking down old blood cells, and digestion.

**Nephron**  One of the microscopic filters inside a kidney that remove waste materials from the blood.

**Neutrophil**  A common type of white blood cell that forms pus.

**Plasma**  In biology, the liquid part of blood.

**Platelet**  One of the microscopic disc-shaped particles found in large numbers in blood that are involved in forming blood clots.

**Pus**  A thick yellow or green liquid made of dead white blood cells and bacteria.

**Pustule**  A spot or pimple on the skin filled with pus. Also known as a zit.

**Rhesus factor**  An antigen found on the surface of some people's red blood cells.

**Scab**  In biology, a crust that forms over a cut or scrape during healing.

**Sickle cell anemia**  A type of anemia caused by distorted red blood cells.

**Vein**  A blood vessel that carries blood flowing toward the heart.

**Vitamin**  One of several chemical compounds needed in small quantities by the body for normal growth and function.

# Index